All

Things

in

Common

Rupert Fike's *All Things in Common* is a multi-voiced account of how a group of hippies and activists took the American Dream further than it had ever gone before—perhaps further than it was ever meant to go—transforming a patch of Tennessee wilderness into a makeshift utopia called The Farm. It interweaves social history and personal history in poems that are readable, quirky, tender and hilarious, full of Fike's trademark dark humor as well as an unfathomable and unreasonable hope for us all that's steeped in the true spirit of the best of American dreaming, just when we need it most.

— Cecilia Woloch, award-winning poet, teacher, and recipient of NEA and Fulbright Foundation fellowships

All
Things
in
Common

Poems from The Farm

Rupert Fike

REDHAWK
PUBLICATIONS

ALL THINGS IN COMMON

ISBN: 978-1-959346-93-7 (Paperback)

Library of Congress Control Number: 2025937757

Cover photos - Copyright (c) Clifford Chappell and The Foundation
Author photo: Colin Potts
Cover Design (Art): Rupert Fike, Winnie Lanham
Book Design: Robert T Canipe

Printed in the United States of America.

First printing 2025.

Redhawk Publications
The Catawba Valley Community College Press
2550 Hwy 70 SE
Hickory NC 28602
https://redhawkpublications.com

-Fanatics have their dreams, wherewith they weave

a paradise for a sect . . .

- John Keats, The Fall of Hyperion

Prologue

From 1971 to 1983 The Farm evolved into America's largest and most visible commune, a social experiment/spiritual school rooted in this country's tradition of utopian experiments.

The core group of 300 came together in San Francisco before migrating to rural Tennessee where they soon grew to over 1000 "voluntary peasants" who held "all things in common" while not only creating their own village but also beginning ambitious relief projects in third-world countries and neglected corners of this country.

And for many years, the vision seemed to be working until the cumulative effects of not taking nominal care of themselves became the community's undoing even as its reputation continued to thrive. The Farm continues today as a reorganized collective on the same Tennessee land. These poems hope to honor all those who dedicated their youth to this great pure effort.

Table of Contents

Convergence, 1968

The West is the best . . . the West is the best . . .
Get here, we'll do the rest.

- *Jim Morrison*

Scattered across the country, waylaid by potent micrograms
    combining with paperback Buddhism,
    they'd stumbled through a portal, the Oneness thing,
    that most burdensome moral code which,
    once touched, becomes brain flypaper,
    unshakeable, a state akin to going mad.

All cultural signposts pointing them here, San Francisco,
    anointed city of redemption where Snyder, Ginsberg,
    and the Beats had wrestled with Eastern ways,
    coming out the other side as Dharma Bums.
    But the city, as they all do, demanded rent,
    union jobs found down at the docks where some
    became skinny-armed longshoremen by day
    so they could sit with teachers by night --
    gurus, dancing Sufis, hash-huffing fakirs --
    a few charlatans of course, but they didn't care,
    they were too busy striving not to strive,

too busy thinking hard about not thinking,

while exhausted from throwing coffee bean

sacks all day down on the waterfront, or worse,

stacking fresh animal hides in the bottom holds

of rust-bucket freighters just in from Juneau.

And it was down at Pier 37 or over on the Oakland docks,

    that's where they often encountered their

    mirrored-selves just in from Ann Arbor, Akron,

    the Lower East Side, fellow pilgrims who'd heard

    that same call, rode the highway west,

    rode the snake west where

    they met their own kind deep

    below the water line, standing in bilge sludge.

    Appropriate, they thought, that they could go

    no lower in the world, and there,

    pleased with this renunciation of hankering

    they peeled apart hides that so recently

    had covered animals running wild

    much as they had so recently run free

    in leafy college towns or grit-grimy 'hoods.

And they came in waves, each newly arrived caste
        looking up to those who had gotten themselves
        here earlier. those who had venerated the Diggers,
        Summer of Love activists, some the same drop-outs
        Joan Didion had interviewed, disdained.

And they sat in stiff rows at halls, ashrams, store-front
        temples, each copying the other's posture --
        back arch, severe chin-tuck, deep exhalations,
        all striving to master *Right Practice*
        when *Beginner's Mind* was sufficient.

Each Zendo's formality suppressing all chit-chat,
        but in the fogged meadows of Golden Gate Park
        or while working deep in the holds of freighters,
        observations were swapped on teachers,
        which path or discipline had the juice,
        the stuff they'd come here to find.

And oddly enough it was an American, a college professor
        whose weekly classes combined the pith of lectures
        with a kind of stand up spiritual shtick.
        They liked this guy. Stephen. He made them laugh.
        He'd ventured even further into the chemical abyss

13

that had turned them inside-out, yet he'd found
his way back to offer unlikely absolution —
all this dissolute ego-pain was but a symptom
of greater purpose looking for its way out.

He said they were part of an ongoing human lineage —
        those who, throughout time, have wondered, *Why?*
        Much as Whitman did when he held up
        that blade of grass and asked, *Whose?*

Stephen's class filling *The Family Dog* Monday nights,
        the dilated-pupils set still rolling in from Seattle
        and Santa Fe, enrolling in his "sudden school,"
        the community becoming too large for the city.
        Plans hatched to buy land back east,
        make a go of it there -- *Mahayana,* the big boat,
        all souls welcome, "bus families" forming,
        money pooled, ancient school buses
        remodeled into rolling nomadic tents.

Oakies-in-reverse, that's what they became,
        pilgrims leaving the city where
        they'd come together, their meetings
        held so close to the Pacific its waves

could be heard slapping Ocean Beach

just across the Great Highway.

Where the continent ran out,

where there was no more West to get to,

its promise of redemption finally kept.

1939 International Harvester School Bus

After safely transporting the children
    of Calavaras County throughout the '40s,
'50s and '60s, it was auctioned off like some

used-up mare to us, three couples and Vishnu
    the dog — seats torn out, bed platform built,
we aimed it to Tennessee . . . across the great divide,

all the other buses with a three-week head start,
    a rolling community we needed to catch
for we were behind them in so many ways.

The International's grille like a prow, a chrome
    ice-breaker crunching through remorseless winter
nights that gelled the engine oil to such a sludge

the little six-volt battery could not budge it unless
    we brought the thing in at night to keep its ions
excited by the wood stove, Vishnu snorting, moving over.

We held hands in a circle on the bed platform,
    a too-long *Om* before each meal, no one
wanting to be the first to stop and admit hunger.

Lentils on the boil, fogging all ten rows of windows,
    photo of Suzuki Roshi over the cutting board,
India-print bedspreads so thin, all Vedic style,

little warmth, carpet scraps glued to the ceiling,
    the flammable work of some deranged Mondrian,
sooty kerosene lamps scorching its dried-out shag.

Morning ritual of siphoning gas to prime the carb -
    gags, octane-breath a class of birth control,
and under one coldest Wyoming sunrise we had to

drain the engine oil then heat it on the stove,
    slow pops coming like lava, a hydro-carbon
soup du jour whose stench drove us outside,

past the chamber pot (careful!), past the bowls that held
    the amoebas of our shared digestive track.
Cramps bent us double. Wind sang through the gaps

of the push-up windows Sierra kids had once pressed
    their snotty noses against. Lamp wicks ran out.
Dark came early. We could hear each other making love.

Hay

We had somehow bought a team of horses
        before we even had hay,
Jon, raised on a Nebraska farm,
        negotiating the deal that included
        their sweat-hardened harness, traces.
Jon working them hard that first day,
        his guttural, *Hyah!!,* shocking us with its force
        (was he being compassionate?),
        the team responding though,
        bowing their necks, digging in,
        dragging a series of nailed together pallets
        (we had no wagons yet either)
        stacked with grain and propane tanks
        down to a protected meadow, the horses
        perhaps pining for some place with wheels.
And after hours of these labors
        an expectation began forming
        in the eyes of the Belgian mares --
        humans were supposed to feed them.
Kathy and I dispatched (we were from the South)
        to the nearest neighbor's trailer,
        Homer Sanders waving us in,

two shotguns leaning in a corner,

tang of gun oil strong, Saturday night,

Gunsmoke on, same as it would have been

at my parents' house, Marshall Dillon

in a flickering black and white shoot-out,

Homer Sanders not turning it down

(perhaps he wanted to watch his show),

forcing me to almost shout the words

I had rehearsed but dreaded saying,

"We need some hay for our horses."

I pulled out a five and waved it around,

 the gauche gesture he chose to ignore.

 Homer had heard about us (the whole county had)

 but he wanted to know more.

 "You'uns gonna have any 'arties?"

 I stared back to him.

 "Arties! " He yelled.

 "Parties," Kathy said. "He's saying, parties."

 "Oh no," I said. "No parties.

 We're a spiritual community."

 (I wasn't yet adept with our party-line.)

 Homer slapping his knee before he got it out,

 "Well if you ain't having no 'arties,

 I ain't got no hay!"

Later, after backing up to his shed,

       I raised our VW bus' rear door for the hay --

       and here was a moment – the end of an interlude

       in our lives, those last San Francisco months

       spent transforming the van into a floating

       purple bedroom - incense, pillows, each item

       in its place, the décor of a striving spirituality.

       And now our bus had been nationalized,

       turned into a hay wagon, dusty bales

       soiling our once-homey world, landing on

       the bedspread with Krishna and cow maids,

       landing on *The Whole Earth Catalog* with

       its much-thumbed promise, *Access to Tools,*

       the wish-book we'd pored over in the city

       buried beneath red-twined hay.

       We would feel the scratch of straw and grit

       of the earth in our sheets tonight,

       the bargain we had longed to make.

Solstice

Before we knew winter would be trouble
we skipped stones across creek pools,
grasshopper games, death to water-striders.
We sketched plans for unroofable domes . . .
all while locals built mountains of oak splits.

Days shortened so slowly we missed our cues,
giardia burps so acrid, we had to hold our nose.
The Mennonites' old mare (thrown in on some deal)
came up lame, her hooves packed tight with thrush,
its chipped-out stench bringing crows thinking, *Carrion!*

Canning jars didn't seal, and out on Highway 20
semis disturbed the peace with their rat-a-tat exhaust.
Wood smoke hung blue, too cold to escape
scrub-oak hollows, folds in a mapped blanket
that this poorest county still taxed.

We sat with studied discipline. We *Ommmmed*
and made sure the Primitive Baptists knew it.
Kerosene leaked on brown rice - we ate it anyway -
Take that, pinworms! Mud rooms boot-clogged.
Fence post buzzards spreading wings to a brief sun.

The miller refused our Deaf Smith County wheat,
too hard for his stones, he said. High lysine, we said.
Boiled wheat berries never once got done.
Sorghum sweetened cereal gave babies the shits.
Wet oak sizzled, put out fires. Sprout jars froze.

We called distant parents from road-house pay phones.
They were off the clock but still accepted our charges
in that curbed world we'd left for these difficult acres.
Mung flour pancake mornings, firewood ax buried
deep under last night's snow . . . but where?

Public Works

When our new road tried to short-cut a field
     at its low point, the thing soon became
ten yards wide from vehicles trying to get around
     other vehicles sunk to their axles in sucking mud.
Pushers pushing ("Monkeys!" our cry to come help)
     tires spinning, the *whirrr, whirrr* of going nowhere,
friction steam, black rubber glaze coating the ruts,
     pushers muck-sprayed by tires, pushers shouting
at the driver, "Easy! Not so much gas! Stop revving it!!"
     Anger-vibes detected in the shouts, a circle forming
to "sort out" the shouters' "subconscious," this a far more
     important endeavor than the material plane issue
of un-sticking trucks and cars, the next vehicle impatient,
     lurching left, gunning it in second, getting stuck
anyway, digging itself deeper with each *Vroom!* --
     cars and trucks now splayed like mid-game dominos
in impassible furrows, a junk yard scene, the short-cut
     road-bed abandoned, shifted to the tree line,
where it should have been in the first place, our deep-rut
     scars left untreated, forgotten out in the pasture
that had flat-out refused to be breached, a once idyllic
     meadow now blighted by our trenches, the pasture

where one family's cattle had peacefully grazed until
    we arrived with well-meaning but rookie intent,
our scar-tissue ruts freezing solid in winter, twisting
    the ankles of any who tried to use them as a path,
our road ruts now like some World War I battlefield
    minus the barbed wire and dead horses, our frozen
gullies filled by winter rains, becoming finger lakes,
    ecosystem of failed intent, warmer spring nights
bringing frog-courting calls out there, inky commas
    soon seen on warm afternoons in the shallows,
inky commas sprouting May legs, stubby tails,
    and we, the *Yahwehs* of this creation, walking kids
out there to squat, point, revel in this miracle –
    tadpoles where they had never been before.

Sunday Morning

Sitters in the dark, hundreds waiting for the sun
    to crest Hickory Hill, the name we've given it
since the land is now ours, so we can call things

whatever we want, a thousand acres paid for
    (okay, mostly from inheritances), this formerly
anonymous pasture now, *Meditation Meadow*,

the reason we're out here Sunday mornings, dark
    giving way to light, songbirds unfazed by such
a sudden array of humans on blankets and pillows,

still working on their practice same as back in the city.
    Coughs and adenoidal hacks part of the mix,
throat-clearings increasing at the first eastern glow,

the meadow's green tinted by fresh amber photons,
    minds trying to stop minds from being minds --
each of us more than anxious for the *Om* to begin

now that our knees have stiffened. Plus we're hungry.
    And never mind that the *Om* is a Hindu chant
tacked on to the end of this neo-Buddhist sitting

with Native-American peyote tea making the rounds,
    Islamic Sufi stories also part of the mix -
cultural appropriation on nobody's radar,

the world's religions like a wine tasting tour
    except we swallow, partake in earnest,
all of us back in love with each other

even though there may have been words Friday
    over the use of a station wagon. But right now
it doesn't matter. All tractor repairs, gate shifts,

out-of-control trippers, clinic duties and brake jobs,
    all that's forgotten as the sun comes up because
this is why we're really here -- to sit on Sunday mornings.

Your Father Is Sober

That's how my mother's letter begins,
her prim hand adding, *Isn't that something?*
after she notes that his AA group meets
in the same church basement my scout troop
used the winter I had such a time with knots.

My father, sober. Hard to take it in, his new-found
civility a bit late for the boy who's now a man,
digging outhouses with a crew on this scrub-oak
ridge, the letter delivered by "Mail Lady" Denise
making her daily rounds on Belle, an aging

Belgian mare we've just bought from a nearby
Amish family, the Yoders, Denise noting the way
my face changed as I read the letter, Denise wanting
my news (she was a bit of a gossip, no one cared),
Denise yanking the reins, "Whoa now, easy, girl!"

But Belle was twitchy, impatient to get back
to the barn and her new treat, sweet feed, molasses
infused oats just the latest way we'd found to spoil her
same as we never had her harnessed and out
in the fields by seven like the Yoders had worked her

forever until we arrived, academics and drop-outs

with no business owning work animals, bohemians

too drunk on our own self-image as noble agrarians

to actually *be* noble agrarians. And yet we were trying,

working on each other as important as working the land.

Denise still wanting to hear my story (whatever it was),

still going, "Whoa, now," still pulling back on Belle.

The horse still trying to turn around, go get fed.

It was a war of wills, a dance, the mare's weight

churning wet ground into mush, a casual power

reminding me of the damage those hooves could do

to human feet, in this case my feet. And so I backed away,

not so much for safety but to avoid Denise's leading

questions as I kept re-reading my mother's last line —

Your father, your father. We're all so proud.

Single Mothers Sorting Beans

Combines think soybeans are the same as rocks,
so we sit here early sorting the two,
wide trays in our laps held slightly askew
bringing wobbles from pebbles and dirt clods
that never grew in a pod, became round.
All while June oils the pressure cooker ring,
and Lyn reads to the kids before they sing,
Thanks, for their oatmeal, oh, the loveliest sound.
And sure, we do daydream, but in the here and now
we sort beans, gossip and fold clean diapers —
Jill's back from The Bronx, I think Tim likes her —
this household dependent on us, our *Tao*

    to feed twenty children (prompt meals a must!)
    bites with no stones, no explosions of dust.

Maggie May

It played non-stop on AM radio the summer we drove
    back roads looking to lease fallow fields for our
sorghum crop - *Old Beatnik* syrup both a cash-flow hope
    and PR strategy — we would raise cane, cook molasses,
turn a profit and somehow come off as "down home."

    Budding capitalists living Marxist ideals, that was us,
knocking on farmhouse doors in paisley-patched jeans.

    And we must have seemed heaven-sent, dusty angels
waving a wad of twenties at hardscrabble locals,
    the radio in our 3/4 ton Ford set to Top 40 Nashville
and Huntsville, my finger quick-hitting the next button
    each time I heard that mandolin intro to Rod Stewart's
condescending kiss-off note to an older Ex.

    I had to stop ole Rod before that most terrible line –
I suppose I should collect my books and get on back to school,

    This seemed cruel and unusual to have to re-examine
life choices you had already made. Four or five times a day.

    What if this whole adventure were indeed ill-advised?
What if it hadn't been wise to sign that *Vow of Poverty,*
    declare *Voluntary Peasant* status with the IRS?
What if I should collect my books and get on back to school?

    Doubts like these were unwelcome, best kept to yourself.

They would only bring you trouble for we were on a mission.

    We were, as we often said, *Doing this thing.*

We wanted the world's attention (Tom Wolfe's "Big Eye,")

    to swoop down on us, make note of our efforts,

visitors now showing up from all over Europe,

    we put them to work, gave them "relativity."

Summer dragged on, I drove crews out to weed the cane,

    the pick-up bed packed with peasants and hoes,

me in the cab with its radio, *Maggie May* still inescapable.

    If I changed the station, and somebody said, "I love

that song," I'd say it was unkind to women – *The morning*

    sun when it's in your face really shows your age.

And this sometimes worked since we closely watched

    each other for any perceived spiritual transgression,

a constant internal competition of moral one-upmanship.

    "Was it kind for him to say that? Was it necessary?"

And though that wasn't my real problem with the song,

    I had them. Check-mate. They grew silent, chastened.

We were full of ourselves, full of caffeinated sodas,

    buzzed on weed, always trying to "straighten" each other,

each of us a participant in this game of altruistic chicken,

    no one wanting to be the first to back down, admit doubt.

Late September came, our sorghum stalks grown juicy,

    and here came what we most loved – to be a small army

of cane-cutters with machetes — *Venceremos!* Just like Cuba!

    And even though we sometimes overcooked or even

downright burned a batch of syrup, the whole venture

    did gain us a grudging acceptance with the locals.

They saw we were not scary. We were not the Manson family.

    We were harmless as pets, perhaps foolish but trying hard,

spending way too much money to be run out of the county.

    Late September came just as Rod had prophesized,

and with it came fall's desperate yellow jackets dive-bombing

    our syrup as it slow-cooked in shallow copper pans.

We spooned them out though a few wings did get through,

    delicate wisps visible only if you held the jar to the sun.

Late September came, we were late stacking firewood,

    and nobody was going back to school. At least not yet.

He Arrived in a Hollowed-Out Studebaker Lark

George, who had sat in a West Coast ashram,
    who hadn't started with weed and acid the way
we had, his ice-floe eyes and russet ponytail
    soon sparking jealousies among the single ladies
where before there'd been none, the men smirking,
    though we, too, were developing a bit of a crush,
positioning ourselves behind him at Sunday services,
    copying his chin tuck, back arch, deep exhalations —
we wanted to at least look like we were meditating.

    We also had eyes for the Lark. You had to give up
all possessions to live here, George fine with that —
    he'd just spent two cross-country months in the thing,
its front bucket seat removed for sleeping purposes —
    and now an actual Studebaker was our newest town car.
Most of our vehicles were pretty much jokes
    prone to flats, overheating, blown head gaskets,
but the Lark never once broke down; it continued
    as though some spiritual warranty were in place,
as though George's Eastern ways still bestowed . . .
    what was it, Tao? Right Practice? Good old grace?
No sooner had it returned from a West Texas
    peyote run than it was off to visit sick Philly parents,

33

the next driver waiting at the gate, tag-team style.

    We changed its oil, sure, but mostly we just let it ride.

Something was going on here, something well into

    the realm of superstition, which we confused with karma.

The Lark's reign continued for months — or was it years?

    A couple came in with a yellow Caprice that briefly

became our new darling until it developed a rod knock.

    They must have quarreled in it, we decided.

The Lark marched on, always in its no-mind state,

    until the day it got rear-ended in Nashville — bent frame.

We pushed it into the bone-yard blackberry thicket

    at the pace of a fallen hero's cortège, and there,

late at night on its pleated back seat, to the song

    of cicadas, teenagers sometimes made out,

Communal Mule

He came concealed in the womb of Mabel,
one of our Belgian mares, the team
we had bought from the canny Amish
who, by law, never part with good horses.
And then one morning there he was, wobbly,
his sapling legs barely supporting such ears,
all of us swiftly in love, the deal's sting
long gone because we were laughing last,
waiting in line to pet him, Barnabus,
the name that so fit, snuff-dipping neighbors
toasting our fortune before, in short words,
they advised he would have to be "shaved"
to be of any use, to not hurt us.

We did not eat meat or even honey,
so to have a pet (what he was) castrated,
well, it just wasn't going to happen.
No, we would surround him with calming love
same as we "fixed up" mental patients
by first throwing away their meds for
we assumed love's power spanned all species
even though we did find ourselves chasing

relapsed bi-polar friends through briary woods,

even though Barnabus soon started in

with first bites, then frog-quick pole-axing kicks

that put his handlers on crutches for weeks.

Soon only the purest girls dared feed him,

but when he kicked one of them that was it.

He was given to a local logger who shaved him,

and, after the procedure, a much-subdued

Barnabus was sometimes seen snaking logs

from hollows where skidders could not go,

mule sightings on wintery roads that made us

stop our truck, and, helpless to do otherwise,

we approached him like blind men, arms forward,

still wary until that first touch between eyes

that regarded us with a glazed calm,

his pungence cueing recalls of gone times,

but our own stink - wood smoke, dope smoke, gear lube –

brought only cold-fog snorts, harness shakes.

Barney was changed. He didn't know who we were.

Ode to the Land

We casually said we'd "bought" these acres when really

    they'd forever been part of the Chickasaw nation

before they got sent on their long walk, they who named

    these ridges for their habit of pulling lightning from the sky,

one terrible bolt taking dear Eugene that second summer

    as he lay on his back, grounded while pulling parts

from a bus near the old Line Shack, a 19th century artifact

    that came with the land, a pioneer way-station whose roof

was maintained through the Depression by moonshiners

    needing dry storage for their sugar, the Line Shack

built long ago as a resting place for travelers on the trail

    leading west from Columbia (President Polk's home)

to the Natchez Trace, twelve miles west, the trail

    that came through "our" land likely traveled by

Meriwether Lewis, Polk, Davy Crockett,

    Ole Davy mayor of nearby Lawrenceburg where DeSoto

had made winter camp with all his men, horses and pigs,

    the Line Shack's trail now one of our numbered roads,

all eventually dropping to ford Big Swan Creek same as

    frontier travelers had done, the Big Swan uncaring,

cutting ever deeper through its limestone bluffs same as

    it will long after any humans stop coming this way.

Lab Ladies

We await your secretions - blood, snot, piss!
And look . . . in the bottom of an old Gerber's jar
here's baby poop, not runny, more like black tar,
its slide revealing parasites (they're hard to miss) —
shigella dudes doing lazy backstrokes
past e-coli hotties beneath our big eye
that's inspecting the Guatemala crew's insides,
friends welcomed home with kisses and tokes,
which is how amoebas take over whole scenes,
plus kid butts on counters help pinworms abound.
The ounce of prevention we preach is quite sound:
"Keep washing your hands!" It's not like we're mean,
    contagion's a drag and has to be fought.
    This place is one body (that's Buddhist thought).

Slab Shack

When the mice started running relays,

squeaking past with babies in their mouths,

we knew a snake was again in the house

that wasn't much of a house at all,

just some salvaged tin nailed over walls

built from vertical planks of bark, slab wood,

the first cuts off logs at our neighbor's sawmill.

His pile was free for the taking except

you had to watch out on the shifting mound,

and you had to state your intended use,

words you regretted once they left your mouth,

once Homer repeated them, *Build a House!?*

as though he had maybe heard you wrong.

Firewood the one acceptable answer.

The slab lost its bark that first winter

revealing a food-chain habitat where

lower-caste insects thrived then attracted

woodpeckers banging out entry holes

perfect for field mice who sniffed out

a hippie kitchen where grain was stored in bags,

where Tupperware was frowned upon

where even *Siddhartha*'s spine had been gnawed

by creatures intent on nesting scraps.

We set no traps for they were sentient beings,

due Buddha's unwavering compassion

same as the silent black snake who made

its rounds, swallowing small warm bodies

while we, the large warm bodies who could

easily have put a hoe through its head, refrained,

not so much in deference to the teachings,

but because we were standing on the bed.

VW Bug Pumps Water

My father is the world's black ribbon of road
    I will never see again, my mother's milk
the clear leaded octane I still consume,
    its refinery stink overpowering delicate wafts,
sassafras and hoary mint here in this hollow,
    my final resting place where I now pump water
because Meriwether Lewis Electric refuses to run
    two miles of poles down to this cistern.
Mary from Michigan drove me here, my new masters
    liking my purr, backing me down a foot path,
jacking me up, welding a double pulley to my left-rear
    brake drum, fitting it with belts so I can power
the pump with my full 40 horses (once I'm in fourth).
    An oil leak from bad push-rod tubes is caught
on cookie tins, my fluids kept from what's precious –
    water so pure it was once the stuff of secret stills,
retired moonshiners pointing out this vale,
    an Edenic site my bad muffler now spoils
once proper rpms create enough psi in the PVC
    to push water into the tower up on the ridge,
my valve clatter, blue exhaust and spilled gasoline
    all drawbacks yet part of the deal – towhees,
tree-frogs and whippoorwills alike repelled by the stink
    and noise of what I yet miss - the open road.

Peyote Tea

Our friends in the desert send us this ration,

buttons so fresh they've soaked through the cardboard

box we claim at the Mount Pleasant bus station.

Danny, the clerk sniffing, "Hoo-wee! Good Lord!"

Here's medicine, sacrament for those tribes

blessed by road chiefs whose ancient rituals

guide circles who sing and chant with the wise

in kivas. Not us though. We're white people.

Yet we do know to remove the fluff poison

before the huge pot of tea wafts its smell

through households on a cold Sunday morning,

our tongue's ego the first to die as it swells

    when the jar moves around this grouping of friends.

    We sip then shudder to a new world, cleansed.

Nicole is Due in Three Weeks

I got myself up to the house, but the Petty Cash Lady
　　won't give me three bucks to go buy a diaper pail.
"We're not doing store-bought pails anymore," she says
　　while handing me a white five-gallon pickle bucket,
one I know was scammed from behind some McDonalds.
　　Second-class citizen – these words run through my head,
not a spiritual thought, but there it is, thank God,
　　part of me still standing up for me, not shutting up.
Jill (that's her name) demonstrates the bucket's snap-on
　　lid "Fly-proof," she says. "Good for hep control."
Like I'm stupid about the flies-to-shit-to-mouth thing.
　　I know the etiology of hepatitis. That's what I don't say.
Too college-snobby for hippie-chick Jill. For this place.
　　I say, "Nice," instead. Don't mean it but say it.
Have to watch my mouth. One smart-off all it takes.
　　Gets straight back to midwives. Trouble. Big "sort out."
"Heard you got salty with the Petty Cash Lady," they'll say.
　　Circle of faces will lean in. Might start crying.
Jill now giving the next guy in line a twenty for some
　　stupid tractor part. Unfair. Social position. Day ruined.
Won't be catching a ride to the Lawrenceburg Big K
　　to walk those harshly-lit aisles I used to hate

before a month in these woods gave shopping an allure.

　　White bucket. Don't want anything scammed for my baby.
Want a fresh diaper pail with pink fluted sides

　　like the ones I've seen other mothers with.
Not dumb though, I know their folks sent them money.

　　Not an option for me. Parents still upset. Mostly from
losing their deposit on the year-abroad program.

　　"You could have been in Lyon," they keep saying.
But no, I saw that story in the *Mother Earth News* —

　　Come have your baby here for free, it said.
Come get a white bucket, it should have said.

　　Nothing to do now but walk back down the chert road.
A truck stops, dust cloud covers me. Don't want a ride.

　　Want to walk. Stew in wronged juices. Me and white
bucket, new possession. One-gift baby shower. Partner.

　　Stop to put my head in it. Cleansing scent of dill so strong
it combines with the scudding clouds and larky birdsong to,

　　I don't know, I start swinging the thing by its handle.
Lah-de-dah. Not the bucket's fault. It's heavy duty, food-grade,

　　blameless, the world's first notice of my baby.

Visitors Tent

The German girls keep saying we're uptight

around sex (this makes the backpackers smile),

and the Gate just called hoping it'll be all right

to send down four more, one named, Love Child,

a creep so transparently on the make

with Big Sur smooth talk, we know he won't work.

We're way too crowded, we tell the Gate,

You should screen these people! Stop sending down jerks.

And once breakfast is done, Jen from LaCrosse

starts chanting while throwing her *I Ching* sticks -

the Oracle says Farm folks aren't her boss,

she won't go pick squash – this group's a bad mix.

    And there goes Love Child, all charm and blonde curls,

    he's already hitting on the German girls.

Copper

In the Scales Shed we watch Mr. Schlanger
    tap the weights he never has to tap
very far because he already knows
    what our '48 Ford flatbed grosses
out at even with a load of junked cars stacked
    two high, three rows of rusted babies chained
down proper, the way Tennessee state troopers
    like to see loads - boomers tight, on the right.
But it's our drums filled with Number One,
    that's where the money is for both of us,
Mr. Schlanger going, "Copper's up, my boys."
    Like we didn't know that already,
like we've been crawling up under old dashboards
    just for fun the past two days, poking our hands
past wasp nests, snipping wire and thick cable,
    burning off the insulation in piles, what brings
the thickest, blackest rolling smoke cloud
    ruining any blackberries in its path,
mounds of burnt-orange revealed, beauty
    somehow greater than just its weight.
But we smile and nod anyway because maybe
    he means Number One just bumped higher

today, and he'll give our barrels the new best rate.

    We're both newcomers, him a Jew, us hippies,

meeting to do scrap-metal business in Columbia,

    Muletown to all CB users, the town so

forever known for its work-animal market,

    Faulkner sent Snopes men here to buy mules.

Columbia, where young Thurgood Marshall

    almost got lynched. But that's another story.

Some days Mr. Schlanger explains the reasons why

    copper has gone so high this summer —

how Anaconda has been nationalized,

    run out by the new government in Chile.

He always spells out this news slowly,

    like he thinks we never read papers,

but sometimes we'll surprise him

    with our leftover New Left opinions —

"Salvador Allende was elected," we say,

    "by the poor people of his poor country,

and he's doing what he thinks best for them!"

    This makes Mr. Schlanger say the word,

Communist, like he's spitting out a seed,

    like the word itself is shame enough.

But weren't you rescued by the Communists?

That's the question we think to ask but don't
because he never mentions his forearm tattoo,
    sweaty blue numbers glistening on hot days.
Besides, why chance pissing him off?
    He might stop giving us the new best quote
for our Number One, the weight that means a big check
    we can take back to our Bank Lady
so she can at least pay the interest on farming loans
    or fund our village technology projects
to make soy milk proteins available to children
    or buy birthing supplies for the midwives
who've just recently put out the word
    in the underground press coast to coast —
If you're pregnant and scared you can come here,
    and we'll deliver your baby for free,
and if you're still confused, we'll give your baby
    a home until you decide what to do.
Roe v Wade are still just words on a docket,
    and stressed young women with growing bellies
are showing up almost every day now,
    more than we ever thought possible.

Mid-July we hit the scrap-car mother-lode --

    old man Tidwell's sloping metal pasture

crammed with Caddies, DeSotos, Packards

    turned this way and that down to Duke's Creek,

some still with their radiators and battery cables,

    frames made from World War II steel - weight!

We figure we can get two, maybe three

    loads a day up onto Mr. Schlanger's scales,

enough of his big checks to supply birthings

    with oxygen tanks, baby masks, preemie stuff.

Two loads a day though turns out to be difficult

    the way old man Tidwell keeps slowing

things down, dogging us around his old hay field,

    making sure we know the complete story

of each wreck, which bad curve and on what pike

    and who all died, and which Jamison boy,

or was it a Henderson . . . "Anyway," he says,

    "Kid got himself stove up a right smart."

Tidwell still shouting even as our boom truck

    hoists a ruined Bonneville then so softly

stacks it on a Dodge that was once some family's car,

    but now it's taking a last highway ride.

It's almost like Tidwell thinks we should know

    the lineage of each wreck, how long it skidded,

as though its weight alone is not enough,

    his stories from a mouth that's framed by twin

chaw trickles etched into reddish-grey stubble,

    his abscessed-teeth breath harsh, an ill-wind

in our faces, a test of our studied politeness.

    We live in two worlds – sitting za-zen Sundays,

Mondays watching Tidwell spit Red Man juice,

    the flow we try not to look at but do.

Buddha's first noble truth, *All is suffering*

    echoed by spray-painted road cautions

nailed to scrub oaks on sharp curves where you

    can't miss them - *Repent! The End is Near.*

The week Salvador Allende is murdered

    or kills himself (CIA either way),

that's the week we're working the dregs

    of Tidwell's field - the copper's long gone,

just short steel, cast iron and blackberries left.

    And by now the guy who works the big magnet

has told us Mr. Schlanger's long story -

    how he hid out in Amsterdam for a year

before getting hauled off to the camps.

    Perhaps he knew the Franks -- we think that

but never ask. Why force such a memory?

Why remove him from his blessed refuge,
these barrels of Number One, his dirt-dauber

    domain in the musty Scales Shed where he
squints at our flatbed, taps two scale weights

    then best of all, writes our new big check.
But sometimes he'll stop in mid pen-stroke

    to look up at the circle of us, seemingly
losing himself in the tangles of our beards,

    so long and unkempt they're rabbinical,
what must connect to some long-ago spark --

    Friday night, distant bells a reminder,
the boy out of breath, flushed, suddenly

    encircled, like today, by stern beards,
a child's footsteps on wet paving stones,

    time's slippage, the lost world of a
Yeshiva boy, late again for Shul.

Front Door

There's a tent meeting over on the Escue's land

so near the Gate house we can hear them belt

out *In the Garden* with a rocking band,

the low-down bass riffs so funky they're felt

in our sternums (what we call, heart chakras) --

compared to their God, our Buddha seems boorish.

They put their tent there hoping to save us,

but the joke's on them - we're a third Jewish.

And look, here's some west coast freaks pulling in,

our cue to start preaching, "This isn't free land!

We meditate, co-operate, depend

on each other." "Yes!" They go, "You're an ashram!"

    But the tent band's so rocking we have to stare --

    it's like they're having more fun over there.

Pumping an Outhouse

First you take an old two by four
 and poke down the pile, a Matterhorn
 rising almost to the seat . . .
but that's the visitor's job, the sad-eyed
 man-child you recruited in the lunch line,
 Alabama country boy eager to escape
 cabbage rows, endless and wormy in the sun.
"Stoop labor," he called it, not his thing.

And you do try to make it sound like fun,
 bumping through the woods
 on the "Shitter Pumper Truck,"
 an old school bus actually, its body
 torched off, replaced with a tank,
 its rear wheels flattening poplar saplings,
 poke weed, mandrake, whatever's
 in the way of backing up close enough
 so the big hose can go down the dark hole.

A muddied path leads down to the tent-house,
 overcrowded and hepatitis quarantined,
 Clorox fumes choking its kitchen,
 last sad attempt to stave off an outbreak.

And while you're showing him
    how to hold the hose
    (half its eight inches has to suck air),
    you caution him to keep his gloves on,
    to not let any flies get in his mouth.

The stink, of course, is considerable,
    but you tell him he'll get used to it
    because you need a good hose man,
    there's pressure from the Clinic Ladies
    to get this one pumped out today.
That's why you keep yelling, "Good job!"
    from the driver's seat where your foot
    is cramping from holding steady rpms
    while he moves the hose left then right
    (but not straight down!).
And when you've done as much as you can,
    poop level now a good bit lower,
    you walk him down to the creek
    for a hand wash, a face splash,
    and this is where the visitor begins reflecting,
    perhaps thinking you wise, grounded
    (everyone here not shy with advice).
He says he can see he's been acting like a child,

that he needs to call his girlfriend

who doesn't know where he is.

They'd had an argument two nights ago,

over nothing he says,

but there had just been no way

for him to say the word, "Sorry,"

so he went out to sit in the car

because that was where she wasn't.

And then he was driving,

driving three hours here . . .

to show her, to show her . . .

He drifts off, distracted same as you

by goldfinches skittering, kicking up leaves,

males chartreuse as tennis balls,

a tribe of escaped parakeets

so delicate they seem shallow,

incapable of knowing what to do

with this spring, this sudden plumage.

Removing a Tripper

Drop City Slim's been staying at the Gate,

an Aquarian hobo quite obsessed with us,

just off his meds and raising such a fuss

he scared a neighbor lady (that sealed his fate).

His time here is over so now it's our gig,

me and Jerome, to start him on his trip

to the Nashville bus station - us taking lip

the whole way – Slim saying we've reneged

on our vow to help all those in crisis.

But wait, you're not peaceful! Look, here's your fare

back to Taos, it's that bus over there.

And here's lunch money -- no need to thank us.

    We stop for some truck parts, brakes for the Mack,

    but when we get home, Slim's beaten us back.

Sterile Pack Lady

Alone on the moonless main road, 2 am,
    stars reflected in puddles, walking to the laundry,
        midwives out of sterile packs, two birthings tonight.
She goes over again who might be doing it —
    Rebecca out on 5th Road? Jeannette from Canada?
        That tall visitor lady with the yangster husband?
Who can keep track anymore? So many showing up.
    No birthing packs left. How can that be? She's sure
        there were three stacked up yesterday. No matter.
She will process the bags of soiled linens waiting
    at the Mat on their special pallet, the bags
        she was going to do first thing tomorrow.
Today, she corrects herself. It's today.
    Tomorrow has become today in the no-moon dark.
        Whippoorwill from somewhere. Lonesome.
And she needs a helper, Glynis going to the Bronx
    center a problem, crisis really. They'd been a team.
        Now it's just her. On this road. Star puddles. Dark.
Full moon would be worse – even more ladies
    might start doing it. And with no packs left . . .
        that would be bad. Crisis. She'd be in trouble.

Big sort-out. Doesn't want a big sort-out.

    Wants to be seen as competent, maybe start

        helping out at birthings, get trained-up.

Then when Jonas gets his radio license,

    They'll be a couple-team, perfect for Guatemala.

        She goes over the speech she will have to give

when she has to break in line at the laundry

    to at least get one washer going right away.

        Same for a dryer. *Sorry*, she will say.

Birthing packs, she will say. *Priority.*

    And once the first load's in a dryer

        she'll run down to the Sorghum Mill,

wipe down the autoclave, lay out wrapping and twine,

    bats circling now, jazzed by the lights she turned on.

        Owl from Schoolhouse ridge hollow perks up,

same as the ones she used to hear at church camp.

    Just her and the night. All the rest asleep.

        She will wash, dry and fold everything,

count out the instruments, bundle it all up the way

    Glynis showed her - so it fits in the autoclave,

        the reddish wrapping like the butcher paper

her mother used to open in the sink. Liver. Yuck.

She'll get two packs done by the time it turns light,

roads coming alive with trucks then, crews hollering.

They'd slept through the night that was hers alone,

but now its bright, she's walking back home,

trying to slip in without the house ladies noticing,

asking for help with the kids' breakfast clean-up.

No. Not her house day. She goes upstairs

and pulls the covers over her head, last night's sleep

forever gone. Won't get it back. House too noisy.

Mind too busy. Should never get down to no packs.

They should have called her sooner, yesterday even.

Sun streaming in. Harsh. Kids yelling downstairs.

Just a nap, that's all. Just a nap.

Soda Run

The boy and I have plans to siphon gas
    from the Petty Cash Lady's Valiant
for a soda run to Dunn's store, home of Dr. Peppers
    and maybe some Nacho-Cheese Doritos
which would make this a double crime since
    we're really not supposed to eat cheese.
But the gas-taking's kind of rationalized since
    we do hold all things in common, right?
Plus the Petty Cash Lady maybe deserves
    this taxation on her tank because
she tore off her muffler again by not
    staying on top of the deep frozen-mud ruts
out on Third-and-a-Half Road, and actually
    it'll be the boy huffing on the hose,
John, a 14 year-old from Chicago, pretty much
    dumped here by his mother, a speed-loving
lap-dancer who read about us, drove here and left
    him at the Gate with slurred promises to return.

And now, ever since the afternoon I helped him

    fix up an old bike, the boy's become my apprentice,

after-school partner in keeping the midwife

    jeeps running (fifteen birthings this month),

the boy an ace at pulling parts, scamming batteries,

    his hands perfect for getting into small places,

the boy always excited for a soda run, the big perk

    of this gig, the boy finding the clear plastic hose,

twirling the thing, doing a whip-dance just as

    my truck CB starts squawking that the midwives

need more examining gloves right now out on 5th road,

    the boy making a face when I answer, "Roger that,"

say I'll be right back and take off without him,

    my gig as an EMT and midwife *aide de camp*

requiring 24/7 devotion -- two packs of gloves picked up

    at the clinic then a skidding stop at the tent-house

where new life is about to enter this world, my words,

    "Knock-knock" soft as I push through the canvas

flap "door" and enter a scene old as humanity – three "ladies"

    on a bed, backlit by four kerosene lamps, another woman

leaning back, emitting groans, a midwife right up in her face --

Gail, no! Don't check out. Hey! Look at me. Look at me!
There. There you are! HI!! No, stay with me! Good girl!

   We're going to get this baby out, okay? Look at me!
Hi! HI!! Stay with me now. Good girl! Want more pillows?

   I give a cough, place the gloves near a smoking lamp
and back out of the energy as though I were leaving royalty.

   The boy has the hose down the Valiant when I get back,
the trick with siphoning is to not get timid with those first two

      big huffs, what gets the gas over the top, to the place
where the laws of physics take over and fill the can.

   But today he's so pumped from the promise of a soda,
his timing's off, and he chokes on a mouthful of regular,

      an outcome that makes me laugh but not him,
his gasoline burps so filling the cab all the way

      to Summertown we have to roll down both windows
in the late afternoon's 40 degrees, Dunn's store packed

      with the regulars, yarn-spinners, coon-hunters,
tire-changers, the front window's stuffed bobcat

      presiding over all, the goal, as always, to just get
your hippie ass in there, buy some sodas and get out,

      but today Ross Dunn is a wee bit tight,
"Heard there's a bunch of Jews down to y'all's camp."

      "Yup, quite a few all right. Two Dr Peppers please."

And I even buy the boy a small box of saltines

　　　to maybe soak up some of the swallowed gas,

but on the way back the soda's carbonation re-starts

　　　his belches, the air so thick with refinery fumes

I say, "No!" when he pulls out a bomber joint

　　　he scammed somewhere. "No, if you light that

you'll blow us both up." The boy smiling, shutting

　　　me up with, "Sacrament," our code name for weed.

And so we do up the bomber spliff even though

　　　there's a rule against smoking with the teens,

the boy and I laughing about mufflers, soybean farts

　　　and "Conservos" (overly "spiritual" adults),

me being two-faced on that account of course,

　　　before it gets quiet as we turn onto Drake Lane.

And that's when I just up and tell the boy

　　　that his mother is not coming back for him,

news I'd overheard at a Gate meeting last night --

　　　how she had called two days ago,

crying, making blubbering excuses for herself.

　　　And what the boy does when I tell him is this:

he just kind of keeps staring out his window

　　　at the succession of our neighbors'

frost-burned fields, their leaning, tar-paper houses

　　　flanked by pyramids of firewood, yard chickens

pecking, requisite junk cars up on blocks and stumps,

    all the while keeping his face turned from me,

and in a voice I can barely make out, he goes,

    "Yeah. . . I knew that already. . . I knew that."

Notes from a Children's Crusade

We've sent two couples to a clinic in Bangladesh
near the railway station where smallpox is making
its last stand on Earth. But we can't support them.

Earthquake-relief crews in Guatemala need PVC fittings
and pipe for water systems (plus *Povan* for parasites) --
four families off to Mobile to paint houses, send wages.

Judges keep giving troubled youth a last chance with us.
Mental patients, newly released from Central State,
somehow finding their way to the Gate House

that has come to resemble a psych ward, so many meds
to keep track of, each case needing its own handler.
Grandparents "sprung" from New Jersey nursing homes

where they were not happy. Late term pregnancies
showing up unannounced, some with unruly boyfriends.
A free ambulance service begun in the South Bronx --

Wall Street Journal headline -- *In Trouble? Call a Hippie!*
New soy dairy projects launched in the Caribbean.
Our best radio crew dispatched to the *Rainbow Warrior,*

a Greenpeace ship soon to be sunk by the French,
our best ambulance off to support Native Americans
on their Longest Walk to DC then The World Court.

And some Sunday mornings after meditation, amid
rumors of a new inheritance coming in, brave souls
will sometimes stand to suggest we spend it on ourselves.

But this never happens, and those who suggest such a thing
are denounced as, *Hinayana*, the small-boat mentality,
when it's *Mahayana*, the big boat, that's gotten us this far.

Late freeze, green bean crop lost in Florida, loan default.
Vanderbilt hospital debt now six figures, their lawyers antsy.
This is how you get in trouble. This is how you go under.

Plan A, Plan B

That our vision could fully support this scene,

keep the basic budget within our means

via solar, the band, books and soybeans

bringing in cash while promoting this thing.

That was Plan A which only got that name

after it crashed, and Plan B was the fix -

crews packed into vans, leaving at six

to sheetrock, do odd-jobs, paint trim and frame,

their Friday paychecks just barely enough

to service the interest, the crews so exhausted

at each week's end, it seemed that we'd lost it,

the dream which at first hadn't seemed so tough –

to build working models for 3rd World nations . . .

but our cash flow was lacking, banks impatient.

On Top of Everything Else

He now has to start a fire in summer . . .
 under the hot-water tank that used to burn
propane. Until the bill could not be paid.

But first he has to hatchet some kindling
 in the middle of this mushroom-damp July.
No dry wood anywhere. On top of everything else.

How had things gotten harder after ten years?
 Didn't the Ingalls family, alone on the prairie,
start to have an easier go by the time

little Laura was a teen? Yes, but her Papa had not
 decided to overstep, begin myriad projects
in far-away locales. Such never occurred to him.

Pa Ingalls stayed within himself, he hadn't started
 a rock band, bought a Greyhound bus and gone
on tour, leaving his family in a struggling state.

Nor had he put, *Out to Save the World,*
 in the destination sign of his bus without
even the slightest wink to ironic intent.

Pa Ingall's aim had remained true – he tilled his
    square-inch field the way Buddha advised,
today's next square-inch chore requiring hot water,

kids needing to be fed on time to avoid trouble,
    one low blood-sugar boy setting off the rest.
Nobody wanting that. And then come hot baths

which will mean another wood fire. No money,
    no propane. Crews sent out to plant trees for cash,
half teenagers. Last-ditch heroic effort. But not enough.

Families leaving every week now. Going away parties.
    Sometimes even with beer. Last good-byes. Haircuts.
Chopping kindling in summer. On top of everything else.

Bonanza Steak House All-You-Can-Eat Buffet

- Columbia, Tennessee, 1982

We pretend not to see the other family
across the room, and they pretend not to see us.
Better this way since we're both breaking
our long-held vow to share fortunes,
hold all things in common.
And so we avert our eyes from those who split
our oak rounds that winter we got the flu,
who took in our kids after a birthing
so we could have alone time with new life.
And we had done the same for them.

We both know we've come here to fatten up
sapling children, fill small stomachs
grown weary of soybeans and sweet potatoes.
We wonder how they got their seven dollars --
ours is the change from buying tractor parts,
just enough for two adult plates, kids eat free.
Change that should have gone back to Petty Cash.
Graft. Corruption. Mendacity. Hunger.

Our girls can't stop staring at the next table —
three men in Farmers Co-op ball caps
sawing on sirloins, the businesslike clink
of their steak knives a somehow exotic noise.

That's meat. Don't stare.
 They're cutting their meat.
 It's cow meat. Don't stare.
 Some people eat cows.
 Well, yes . . . they're Squares.
 But they're honest Squares.

We go back for seconds still averting
our eyes from the other family because
now there's subconscious between us,
what we had once vowed to not allow,
to always talk out, rob it of its power.
But we don't do that anymore,
we've gone back on the agreements.
We just keep eating while floating plans
to leave and start our life over again.
All while thinking we're bad when really we're not.

Except we *are* bad
for there are single mothers
back in our deep woods who can't
drive here to heap their children's plate
with limitless portions from this neon-lit
sneeze-guarded dream-world —
veggies, casseroles, salads, desserts!
And so there has come to be classes
among us, what was not supposed to happen.
The thing is broken, and we can't fix it.

We had passed our twenties in the '70s,
daily life growing harder the past few years,
more sanctuary cases showing up each day,
some starry-eyed and able. Others not.
Our clothes, lives and lungs now coated
by a fine sheen of orange road dust.
Our grand plan to create third-world village
systems for water, soy protein and solar —
all that had succeeded except we forgot,
along the way, to take care of ourselves,
we who had grown up well-off and now missed it,
we who had volunteered to be modern-day serfs,

fashion-forward peasants with a vision,

the choice our children hadn't made for themselves,

children who still can't stop gawking

at the next-table meat-cutters with clinking knives

even as we spoon extra banana pudding

onto the girls' plates while explaining its mystery —

Those are baked egg whites on top.

Good, huh? My granny used to make this.

Eggs fluff up like that when you beat them.

No, with an egg-beater.

It's a thing that goes round and round.

No, eggs aren't yucky anymore.

Stop staring at those men.

Here, have some more.

A Former Midwife Returns To Walk the Cemetery, 1998

- The Farm is the fountainhead of direct-entry midwifery.

-Jessica Mitford,

An American Way of Birth

She has long since moved on
to power-point presentations
and Business Class seating,
her formerly never-styled hair
now with highlights, much as
this hacked-out clearing
has landscaped itself from
the expectations that come
with burying-grounds.

All of her catches are grown now,
past college or parents themselves,
hundreds delivered in these woods
where even the nearby Amish
buggied in dilating bonneted women
who pushed, panted and gripped her arms
same as the resident mothers
who were a good bit less stoic.

74

She stops at the grave of an infant
who took its allotted gulps of air
before ending up here, the world
not yet ready to make it a place,
or maybe the world knew
something no one else did.
The midwives' statistics are beyond reproach,
yet a few, as always, just don't make it.

Here's one beneath a dogwood
who once took a hot ride with her,
the homemade Chevy ambulance filled
first with shouted commands then prayers,
the chert road's fine dust swirling,
finding its way inside to settle
on the still-wet dead
same as the sweat-drenched living —
a reddish-tinted planet perhaps
glimpsed in a life's single shutter click.

She speaks to a baby she held one night,
her touch the only touch it ever felt.

She passes on love from its parents
and news of its grown siblings' feats.
The child's grave nestled amongst those
who had come to the land so long ago,
some staying to grow old,
others leaving then returning
to this clearing as per their wishes --
ashes, bodies, headstones, cenotaphs.
And if she knew them in their shared
California youth, they remain eternally young
same as these babes will always be babes –

All that lives must die,

passing through nature to eternity . . .
the remembered Shakespeare a comfort
as she turns to go and leave them again
with this clearing all to themselves.

Acknowledgments

Thanks to the following publications in which these poems first appeared:

"He Arrived in a Hollowed-Out Lark"—*The Sun*

"Single Mothers Sorting Beans"—*Calamaro*

"Slab Shack"—*Flycatcher*

"Copper"—*The Dead-Mule School of Southern Literature*

"Nicole is Due in Three Weeks"—*The Power of the Feminine "I"*

"Slab Shack"—*Flycatcher; Hello the House*

"Communal Mule"—*Lotus Buffet*

"Soda Run"—*TrapDoor*

About the Author

Rupert Fike left the University of Georgia in his junior year to work in the Peace and Civil Rights movements of the late 1960s. He and his wife, Kathy, moved to San Francisco, where they helped found The Farm, a spiritual community in middle Tennessee. They have two daughters and three grandchildren and currently reside in Clarkston, Georgia.

Rupert Fike's second collection of poems, *Hello the House (Snake Nation Press)* was named as one of the "Books All Georgians Should Read, 2018" by The Georgia Center for the Book. He was the finalist as Georgia Author of the Year after his first collection, *Lotus Buffet* (Brick Road Poetry Press, 2011). His stories and poems have appeared in *The Southern Poetry Review, The Sun, The Main Street Rag, Kestrel, Scalawag Magazine, The Georgetown Review, A&U America's AIDS Magazine, The Flannery O'Connor Review, Duende, The Buddhist Poetry Review, Natural Bridge* and others. He was the editor of *Voices From The Farm*, a non-fiction title from *The Book Publishing Company, 1997.* He also has a poem inscribed in a downtown Atlanta plaza.

www.ingramcontent.com/pod-product-compliance
Lightning Source LLC
Chambersburg PA
CBHW031601060326
40783CB00026B/4174

* 9 781959 346937 *